AMAZING
SCIENCE

Splish! Splash!

A Book About Rain

by **Josepha Sherman**   illustrated by **Jeff Yesh**

Thanks to our advisers for their expertise, research, knowledge, and advice:

Mark W. Seeley, Ph.D., Professor of Meteorology and Climatology
Department of Soil, Water, and Climate
University of Minnesota, St. Paul

Mike Graf, M.A., Instructor of Child Development
Chico (California) State University

Susan Kesselring, M.A., Literacy Educator
Rosemount-Apple Valley-Eagan (Minnesota) School District

PICTURE WINDOW BOOKS
Minneapolis, Minnesota

Managing Editor: Bob Temple
Creative Director: Terri Foley
Editors: Sara E. Hoffmann, Michael Dahl
Editorial Adviser: Andrea Cascardi
Copy Editor: Laurie Kahn
Designer: Nathan Gassman
Page production: Picture Window Books
The illustrations in this book were rendered digitally.

Picture Window Books
5115 Excelsior Boulevard
Suite 232
Minneapolis, MN 55416
1-877-845-8392
www.picturewindowbooks.com

Copyright © 2004 by Picture Window Books
All rights reserved. No part of this book may be reproduced
without written permission from the publisher. The publisher
takes no responsibility for the use of any of the materials or
methods described in this book, nor for the products thereof.

Printed in the United States of America.

Library of Congress Cataloging-in-Publication Data
Sherman, Josepha.
Splish, splash! : a book about rain / by Josepha Sherman ;
illustrated by Jeff Yesh. v. cm. — (Amazing science)
Includes bibliographical references and index.
Contents: Rainclouds—Sunlight and water vapor—
The water cycle—Rain on the Earth—
We need rain—Dangers from rain—Drought.
ISBN 1-4048-0095-6 (hardcover)
ISBN 1-4048-0339-4 (paperback)
1. Rain and rainfall—Juvenile literature. [1. Rain and rainfall.]
I. Yesh, Jeff, 1971— ill. II. Title.
QC924.7 .S48 2003
551.57'7—dc21
2003004703

Table of Contents

4

Splish, splash!

Boots, bikes, and puppy paws swish through rain puddles. Dirt turns into mud. Streets shine like mirrors. Look up and watch the raindrops sail down from gray clouds.

How Rain Falls

Rain starts out as tiny droplets of water.

These droplets hang in the clouds.

When the droplets bump into one another,

they join together and grow larger and heavier.

Finally, they fall from the clouds as rain.

The Water Cycle

Rain is part of the earth's water cycle.

This water cycle never stops.

The cycle begins when sunlight heats
the water from oceans, lakes, and rivers.

As the water warms, some of it turns
into water vapor. This is air with water drops
so small you can't see them. The water vapor
rises higher and higher with currents of air.
As the vapor gets higher, it cools and turns into
tiny droplets. The droplets form mist or clouds.

9

The clouds bring rain that falls to the earth.

The rain soaks into the ground.

It also travels to oceans, lakes, and rivers.

Vapor turns to clouds

Rain falls from clouds

Water turns to vapor

Some of the water evaporates.
Then the cycle starts again.

Rain on the Earth

Rain falls on most of the earth. In tropical countries, the air is often humid. It is loaded with invisible water vapor.

Some tropical areas get rain all year. Others get very heavy rain off and on. Giant rain forests thrive in the rainfall.

In other areas, deserts cover the land.
These areas are mostly hot and dry.
In desert areas, it does not rain often.
When it does rain, it can be a downpour!

We Need Rain

Rain gives us fresh water to drink.

It helps trees and plants grow, giving us fruits and vegetables to eat. Rain cleans the air by washing away dust and dirt.

Take a shower. Wash your clothes.
Drop an ice cube into a glass.
All the water we use comes from rain.

Dangers from Rain

Too much rain can make rivers overflow. Rainstorms can flood streets and turn the ground to mud. Dangerous mudslides sweep down hills. They crush houses and block highways.

Rain droplets can freeze high in the air.
Then they fall to earth as hail.
Hailstones bang against roofs
and windows. Thick hail can
cover streets and sidewalks like snow.

Drought

Too little rain for too long can cause a drought.

Rivers and lakes dry up. Plants wither and die.
Without plants, animals grow hungry.
In a severe drought, the ground becomes dusty
and cracks open.

Splish!

Splash!

Water pours from a faucet into the bathtub.

The water in the tub first came from rain.

The water that cleans your face and hands first fell to earth from a cloud. Rain gives us water to drink, to clean, and to play.

You Can See the Water Cycle

What you need:

- water
- a small paper cup
- a plastic sandwich bag that can be sealed
- tape

What you do:

1. Make sure you have an adult help you.

2. Put a small amount of water in the paper cup.

3. Place the cup in the bag.

4. Close the bag.

5. Tape the bag with the cup of water inside of it to a window that lets in a lot of sun. Be careful not to spill the water.

6. Watch the bag for a few days. What happens to the water in the cup when it sits in the sun? What happens to the bag?

Will It Rain Soon?

Some people believe there are sayings that will help them discover whether it will rain. These sayings are interesting, but they are not always true. Below are some sayings about rain. Have you heard any other sayings about the weather?

- If there is a white halo around the sun or moon, it will rain soon.

- When frogs croak a lot, it means a storm is coming.

- When dogs eat grass, the weather will be rainy.

- If a squirrel stores a lot of nuts, expect a rainy or snowy winter.

- When cows lie down in a field, rain is on its way.

Glossary

droplet—a small drop of water

drought—when the land is dry because of too little rain. A drought can be severe, or so mild that you hardly notice it.

hail—frozen water droplets that fall to earth as hard balls of ice

humid—when the air is full of water vapor. In tropical places, the air can be so full of water vapor that it feels thick.

rain forest—a tropical forest where a lot of rain falls

tropical—an area that is warm enough for plants to grow all year

water vapor—water in the form of a gas that you cannot see

To Learn More

At the Library

Branley, Franklyn M. *Down Comes the Rain*. New York: HarperCollins Publishers, 1997.

Owen, Andy. *Rain*. Des Plaines, Ill.: Heinemann Library, 1999.

Schaefer, Lola M. *A Rainy Day*. Mankato, Minn.: Pebble Books, 2000.

On the Web

For Kids Only: Earth Science Enterprise
http://kids.earth.nasa.gov
For information on NASA and how its scientists study air, water, and land

The National Severe Storms Laboratory's Weather Room
http://www.nssl.noaa.gov/edu
For fun, basic information on weather for kids, parents, and teachers

Fact Hound
Fact Hound offers a safe, fun way to find Web sites related to this book. All of the sites on Fact Hound have been researched by our staff.
http://www.facthound.com

1. Visit the Fact Hound home page.

2. Enter a search word related to this book, or type in this special code: 1404800956.

3. Click on the FETCH IT button.

Your trusty Fact Hound will fetch the best sites for you!

Index

HRINX +
551
.577
S

DISCARD

SHERMAN, JOSEPHA
SPLISH! SPLASH!

RING
12/06